Mark Twain

by Valerie Bodden

Content Consultant
Joseph Csicsila
Professor, Department of English
Eastern Michigan University

CORE
LIBRARY

Published by ABDO Publishing Company, PO Box 398166, Minneapolis, MN 55439. Copyright © 2013 by Abdo Consulting Group, Inc. International copyrights reserved in all countries. No part of this book may be reproduced in any form without written permission from the publisher. The Core Library™ is a trademark and logo of ABDO Publishing Company.

Printed in the United States of America,
North Mankato, Minnesota
112012
012013

♻ THIS BOOK CONTAINS AT LEAST 10% RECYCLED MATERIALS.

Editor: Kari Cornell
Series Designer: Becky Daum

Cataloging-in-Publication Data
Bodden, Valerie.
 Mark Twain / Valerie Bodden.
   p. cm. -- (Great American authors)
Includes bibliographical references and index.
ISBN 978-1-61783-719-7
1. Twain, Mark, 1835-1910--Juvenile literature. 2. Authors, American--19th century--Biography--Juvenile literature. 3. Humorists, American--19th century--Biography--Juvenile literature. I. Title.
818/.409--dc23
[B]

                                                   2012946801

Photo Credits: AP Images, cover, 1, 7, 37; Private Collection/© Look and Learn/The Bridgeman Art Library, 4; North Wind/North Wind Picture Archives, 9, 16, 28, 32, 39; Shutterstock Images, 10, 35; Public Domain, 14; Red Line Editorial, 15, 41; Bettmann/Corbis/AP Images, 19, 27; Library of Congress, 22, 26, 45; Eric Risberg/AP Images, 25

CONTENTS

CHAPTER ONE

Following the River

On March 4, 1857, a young Samuel Clemens stood in the pilothouse of the *Colonel Crossman*. For Clemens, who would later be known as Mark Twain, this would be his first voyage as a cub, or apprentice, pilot on the great Mississippi River. As the steamboat left New Orleans for its trip upriver, pilot Horace Bixby turned the wheel over to Clemens. His heart racing, Clemens scanned the river.

Samuel Clemens steers a steamship during his time as a pilot on the Mississippi River.

Learning a Lesson

Once Clemens was piloting a stretch of river that he knew was deep. Yet, his leadsman reported that the river was getting very shallow. Clemens panicked. He shouted to reverse the engines. At that moment, pilot Horace Bixby told Clemens that the shallow report was a prank. Clemens was embarrassed. He had learned an important lesson about trusting his own knowledge of the river.

His steamboat seemed much too close to the other ships in the harbor. So Clemens nervously steered the ship toward the middle of the river. He felt proud that he had steered the boat into a safe position. But Bixby began to yell and took back the wheel. The pilot explained that the boat had to stay close to the shore when going upstream to avoid a reef. This was just one of many lessons Clemens learned while he trained to be a pilot.

Learning the River

Clemens had to learn 1,200 miles of the Mississippi forward and backward. That meant knowing the water depth and dangers at every point on the river. He had

Later in life, Clemens became famous for his writings. People often recognized him in his white suits and red socks.

to know how to guide the ship through daylight, thick fog, and darkness. And he had to be able to tell when the river was rising and when it was falling.

At times Clemens worried that he would never learn the river well enough to pilot it by himself. But before his two-year training period was over, he had begun to feel more relaxed. Now the river was as easy for him to read as a book.

Sam's brother, Henry Clemens, shown here around 1855

FURTHER EVIDENCE

There is quite a bit of information about Mark Twain in Chapter One. If you could pick out the main point, what would it be? What evidence was given to support that point? Visit the Web site below to learn more about Twain. Choose a quote from the Web site, and write a few sentences explaining how the quote relates to this chapter.

Old Times on the Mississippi
www.pbs.org/marktwain/scrapbook/02_old_times/index.html

Later in life, Clemens became famous for his writings. People often recognized him in his white suits and red socks.

to know how to guide the ship through daylight, thick fog, and darkness. And he had to be able to tell when the river was rising and when it was falling.

At times Clemens worried that he would never learn the river well enough to pilot it by himself. But before his two-year training period was over, he had begun to feel more relaxed. Now the river was as easy for him to read as a book.

The Pilot's Life

On April 9, 1859, Clemens received his pilot's license. With it came status and a good amount of money—$250 a month. Clemens was happy with his new job. He planned to remain a pilot the rest of his life. But when the American Civil War began in 1861, steamboat traffic on the river came to a stop. It was time for Clemens to move on. He would always remember his time as a steamboat pilot.

Tragedy on the River

Sam was happy with his work on a riverboat. He told his younger brother Henry he should work on a boat as well. So in 1858, Henry began to work on the steamboat *Pennsylvania*. On June 13, Henry was aboard the *Pennsylvania* when its boilers blew up. Clemens rushed to the hospital where survivors had been taken. He found his brother badly burned. Eight days after the accident, Henry died. Clemens blamed himself.

CHAPTER TWO

Boyhood Paradise

Samuel Langhorne Clemens was born on November 30, 1835, in the small town of Florida, Missouri. He was the second youngest of seven children born to John Marshall and Jane Lampton Clemens.

In 1839 when Sam was four, his family moved to the town of Hannibal, Missouri, on the Mississippi River. To Sam and his friends, Hannibal was paradise.

As a young boy, Samuel Clemens lived in this house in Hannibal, Missouri. Many of the ideas for his later stories came from his life experiences in this Mississippi River town.

Risk Taker

As a young boy, Sam Clemens took many risks. While swimming in the summer, he often found himself near drowning, only to be saved by someone on shore. Once in the winter, he went ice skating on the Mississippi when the ice was breaking up. And when a measles epidemic hit the town, he climbed into bed with a friend who had the disease. He caught it himself and nearly died.

The youngsters spent their days watching steamboats, swimming, fishing, and pretending to be pirates. At night they tested their bravery by sneaking out to visit the graveyard.

Living with Slavery

Sam grew up in the years before the American Civil War, when Missouri was a slave state. Like most white Southerners at the time, Sam saw slavery as a normal part of everyday life. His family owned a slave for a time. He also spent nearly every summer at the farm of his uncle John Quarles, who owned 30 slaves. There Sam loved to listen to Uncle Dan'l, an old slave who told stories about ghosts and talking animals.

New Responsibilities

In 1847 Sam's father died of pneumonia. He left his family with very little money. In order to help the family, Sam began to work after school and during the summer. Sam was only 11 years old. The next year, Sam became a printer's apprentice at the local newspaper.

In 1850 Sam went to work for his older brother, Orion, who had started a newspaper called the *Hannibal Journal*. While working there, Sam discovered his love of writing. Orion soon acquired the *Western Union* newspaper, and the *Hannibal Journal* became part of that publication. Sam's first story was published in the *Western Union* on January 16, 1851. In a lighthearted way, he wrote about how a coworker tried to save items from the office when the grocery store next door caught fire.

The Traveler

By 1853 Sam was ready for a change. He wanted to travel the country. He spent time in Philadelphia,

A 15-year-old Sam Clemens holds the metal uppercase letters used to print his name. At the time, printers set each letter for every word by hand into lines of type. Several lines of type made up a page of text.

Pennsylvania; Washington DC; Keokuk, Iowa; Saint Louis, Missouri; and Cincinnati, Ohio. Often he'd work for a short time as a printer before moving on.

In 1857 he became a steamboat pilot on the Mississippi River. He spent the next four years traveling up and down the river he had played in as a young boy.

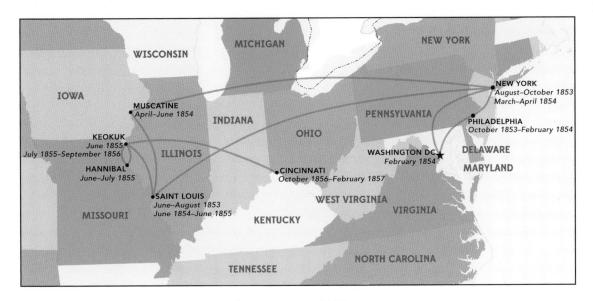

Sam Clemens's Travels, 1853–1857

After leaving his hometown of Hannibal in 1853, Sam Clemens lived in and visited a number of cities before becoming a steamboat captain. This map tracks Sam's travels. Look at the map, and think about how he moved from place to place. Do you think he traveled by steamboat or by train? Write 200 words describing how Sam traveled the country.

His riverboat career ended at the beginning of the American Civil War. Sam spent two weeks in a Confederate militia unit. After the group broke up, Sam decided it was time to go west.

CHAPTER THREE

Becoming Mark Twain

In September 1861, Sam Clemens moved to Virginia City, Nevada. He worked as a local reporter for the *Virginia City Territorial Enterprise*. While writing for the *Territorial Enterprise*, Clemens decided to try out a new pen name. He had earlier signed some of his stories as W. Epaminondas Adrastus Blab or Thomas Jefferson Snodgrass. In 1863 he became Mark Twain. He took the name from

A hand-colored photograph of a young Mark Twain in 1864, when he was a reporter for the Virginia City Territorial Enterprise

The Petrified Man

When there wasn't enough interesting news to report in the *Territorial Enterprise*, Twain made some up. On October 4, 1862, he wrote a news story about a petrified man. He claimed the man had been found in a seated position. He had become stuck to the ground by limestone sediments. Newspaper editors around the country reprinted the story. They believed it was true.

his steamboating days. "Mark twain" indicated a water depth of 12 feet—a depth that was safe for a steamboat's passage. Soon friends old and new called Samuel Clemens Mark Twain.

Finding Fame

In May 1864, Mark Twain moved to San Francisco, California. He took a job as a local reporter for the *Daily Morning Call*. He also wrote for the *Golden Era* and *Californian*, two literary journals.

That December Twain took a trip to a friend's mining camp, where he heard a retelling of a popular old tale. In the story, a man bets a stranger that his frog is the best jumper in the county. The stranger fills the frog with lead shot to keep it from jumping

In this cartoon drawing from 1872, Mark Twain is shown riding on the jumping frog from his famous story.

and wins the bet. Twain returned to San Francisco and wrote the story. He added a serious narrator to make the story funny. "Jim Smiley and His Jumping Frog" was first published in the *New York Saturday Press* on November 18, 1865. Soon it was reprinted in newspapers across the country. The story was later renamed "The Celebrated Jumping Frog of Calaveras County." It brought Twain almost instant fame.

Hawaiian Adventure

On the heels of his successful short story, Twain arranged to write a series of travel letters for the *Sacramento Union*. The letters would be based on a trip to the Sandwich Islands, the independent kingdom that would later become Hawaii. He arrived there in March 1866. Over the next four months, he wrote letters based on the islands' beautiful scenery, the kingdom's people, and their culture.

When he returned to the United States, Twain went on his first lecture tour. Audiences loved his humorous tales of his adventures in the Sandwich Islands. He was on his way to becoming known as the funniest man in the nation.

STRAIGHT TO THE SOURCE

Mark Twain's funny tale of "Jim Smiley and His Jumping Frog" became a famous short story. In this part of the story, the stranger fills Smiley's frog "Dan'l" with quail shot before the men get ready to race their frogs:

> So he set there a good while thinking and thinking to hisself, and then he got the frog out and prized his mouth open and took a teaspoon and filled him full of quail shot . . . Smiley he went to the swamp and slopped around in the mud for a long time, and finally he ketched a frog, and fetched him in, and give him to this feller, and says:
>
> "Now, if you're ready, set him alongside of Dan'l [the frog].". . . Then he says, "One—two—three—jump!" and him and the feller touched up the frogs from behind, and the new frog hopped off, but Dan'l didn't give a heave.

Source: Mark Twain. "Jim Smiley and His Jumping Frog."
New York Saturday Press, November 18, 1865. Print.

Consider Your Audience

Review this passage closely. Consider how you would adapt it for a different audience, such as your parents, your principal, or younger friends. Write a blog post conveying this same information for the new audience. How does your new approach differ from the original text and why?

CHAPTER FOUR

A Literary Life

On June 8, 1867, Twain boarded the steamship *Quaker City* in New York. He set out across the Atlantic Ocean. He spent the next five months touring Morocco, France, Greece, Italy, Russia, Egypt, and Palestine. Along the way, he sent travel letters back to the *Alta California*, the *New York Tribune*, and the *New York Herald*.

Early in his career as a writer, Mark Twain sits for a photograph with writer and war correspondent George A. Townsend, left, and Buffalo Express editor David Gray, right.

New Books

In 1872 Twain published a new book, called *Roughing It*, about his adventures in the American West. This book helped shape the West's reputation as a wild, lawless land. In 1874 Twain wrote his first novel, *The Gilded Age*, with Charles Dudley Warner.

Married Life

On his trip aboard the *Quaker City*, Twain met a young man named Charley Langdon. Soon after the trip, Charley introduced Twain to his sister Olivia (known as Livy). Although Livy was 10 years younger than Twain, he was smitten. He wrote Livy 184 letters over the next 17 months. On February 2, 1870, they married.

The couple moved to Buffalo, New York. Livy's parents bought them an elegant house. They also lent Twain money to buy part ownership in the *Buffalo Express*, where Twain became managing editor. On November 7, 1870, Livy gave birth to a son, Langdon.

In October 1871, Twain and Livy moved to Hartford, Connecticut. On March 19, 1872, Livy gave

A photograph of Mark Twain's wife, Olivia Langdon, sits near the book *Mark Twain's Letters: Vol. 4*, which was written at the time of their wedding.

birth to a daughter named Olivia Susan. They called their new daughter Susy. Three months later, Langdon died of diphtheria. He was only one year old. Twain blamed himself for letting the boy get too cold during a carriage ride.

In 1874 Twain and his family moved into a large and expensive three-story home in Hartford, Connecticut. The family would live there for the next

Mark Twain and his family lived in this house in Hartford, Connecticut, from 1874 until 1891.

17 years. In this home, two more daughters were born: Clara in 1874 and Jean in 1880.

A Boy's Tale

Twain and his family spent most summers at his sister-in-law's estate, the Quarry Farm. It was here that Twain completed *The Adventures of Tom Sawyer* in 1875. The story was about a young boy named Tom Sawyer growing up in a town along the Mississippi River. It had many autobiographical elements. Tom Sawyer's hometown is based on Twain's own boyhood

In an illustration from the 1910 edition of *The Adventures of Tom Sawyer*, Tom whitewashes a fence while Huckleberry Finn looks on.

home of Hannibal. The character of Tom Sawyer is a mixture of Twain and a boyhood friend. The character of Huckleberry Finn was much like Tom Blankenship, whose father was known throughout Hannibal for drinking too much. When it was first published in 1876, *Tom Sawyer* did not sell as well as Twain's earlier books. But since then, it has become his most successful book.

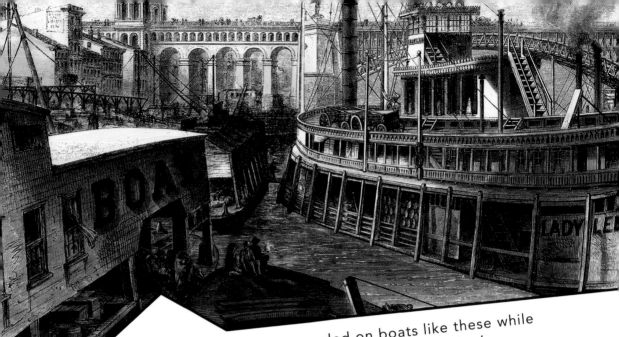

Mark Twain would have traveled on boats like these while doing research for his book *Life on the Mississippi*.

Traveling and Writing

In 1878 Twain and his family set sail for Europe. They traveled for more than a year. They visited Germany, Switzerland, Italy, Paris, and England. When he returned home, Twain published a book about the trip called *A Tramp Abroad*.

Twain then finished a book he had started writing before going to Europe. *The Prince and the Pauper* is a children's novel set in the 1500s in England. In it, two young boys, a prince and a pauper, accidently trade places. Each then learns what the other's life is like.

In 1882 Twain took a trip down the Mississippi River. Along the way, he took notes for a new book called *Life on the Mississippi*. The book included his new experiences plus articles he had already published about his life as a steamboat pilot.

Family Man

Although often away from home, Twain was a devoted husband and father. He read or made up bedtime stories for his daughters. He also played games, including charades, with them. At Christmastime, he dressed up as St. Nick. And after Twain wrote *The Prince and the Pauper*, the whole family performed the tale for friends.

Creating a Masterpiece

After his trip back down the Mississippi, Twain decided to return to a story he had begun in 1876. This sequel to *The Adventures of Tom Sawyer* was called *Adventures of Huckleberry Finn*.

In this novel, Huck runs away from home and travels down the Mississippi River with an escaped slave named Jim.

When *Huckleberry Finn* was published in the United States in 1885, many critics were offended by the book's rough language and questionable morals. Huck Finn tells his story in the vernacular, or everyday language, of his Southern hometown. Today the novel is regarded as Twain's best work. *Huckleberry Finn* is praised for its language and for how it deals with issues of race.

In *Adventures of Huckleberry Finn*, Huck becomes friends with the runaway slave Jim, but Huck has been raised to think slavery is right. He believes he is sinning by not returning Jim to his owner. In this part of the novel, Huck questions whether he is doing the right thing by not turning Jim in:

> *Jim said it made him all over trembly and feverish to be so close to freedom. Well, I can tell you it made me all over trembly and feverish, too, to hear him, because I begun to get it through my head that he was most free—and who was to blame for it? Why, me. I couldn't get that out of my conscience, no how nor no way. . . I tried to make out to myself that I warn't to blame, because I didn't run Jim off from his rightful owner; but it warn't no use, conscience up and says, every time, "But you knowed he was running for his freedom, and you could a paddled ashore and told somebody." That was so—I couldn't get around that, noway.*

> *Source: Mark Twain. Adventures of Huckleberry Finn. New York: Charles L. Webster, 1885. Print. 123.*

What's the Big Idea?

Read this excerpt from *Adventures of Huckleberry Finn* carefully. What is the main point of the passage? Name two or three details that support that point.

CHAPTER FIVE

Final Adventures

By the mid-1880s, Twain was the richest author in America. Yet he was always looking for ways to make even more money. He loved new inventions. He invested in a steam generator, a steam pulley, and a new engraving process. In each case, he lost money. Twain's biggest investment was in a new typesetter invented by James W. Paige. By 1889 he had invested more than $150,000 in the

In this hand-colored photograph, Mark Twain visits his publisher in New York in 1900.

The Inventor

Twain was fascinated by the inventions of the 1800s. He even came up with several inventions of his own. One was an elastic strap to hold a man's pants up. Another was a children's history game. His only mildly successful invention was a self-pasting scrapbook. The pages of the book were coated with a glue that became sticky when moistened.

machine, which would ultimately fail.

Losing money on failed investments was difficult for Twain and his family. He had pledged to retire from writing. But he needed money. So in the early months of 1891, Twain quickly wrote *The American Claimant*. His new novel featured some of the same characters as *The Gilded Age*. Unfortunately, few people bought the book.

Twain soon decided that his family could save money by moving to Europe. Such a move had also been recommended by Livy's doctors for health reasons. She had been having what doctors called a "heart disturbance." On June 6, 1891, the family

From 1896 to 1897, Mark Twain lived in this Victorian house in the Chelsea neighborhood of London, England.

set out on their overseas journey. They spent time in France, Switzerland, and Germany. To earn money quickly, Twain wrote a series of travel articles. But the writing wasn't easy. Twain was suffering from severe rheumatism in his right arm.

Back to Writing

After several months, Twain's rheumatism began to ease. In 1892 he began writing a new novel called

The Tragedy of Pudd'nhead Wilson. A sharp satire, this novel returns to the world of Twain's boyhood South. It reveals what happens when a slave mother switches her light-skinned slave baby with the baby born to her master's wife.

Twain also began writing a historical book called *Personal Recollections of Joan of Arc.* He based the book's portrait of Joan of Arc largely on his oldest daughter Susy.

Around the World

In April 1894, Twain's publishing company had to declare bankruptcy. Although he was not legally required to pay back all of the company's debts, Twain was determined to do so. The fastest way for him to earn money was with a lecture tour. This time he brought Livy and their daughter Clara with him. Susy and Jean remained in the United States with family and friends. Twain gave lectures throughout the northern United States and Canada. In August 1895,

Mark Twain is shown here with his wife, Livy, *center,* and one of his daughters, Clara, in 1900.

he set sail for Australia, New Zealand, Ceylon, India, and South Africa.

After giving more than 100 lectures in just under a year, Twain arrived in England. There he, Livy, and Clara were to meet Susy and Jean. They soon learned, however, that Susy was too ill to travel. On August 19, 1896, Twain got word that his oldest daughter had died at age 24 of spinal meningitis. He was devastated. Once again he blamed himself.

Solace in Work

After Susy's death, Twain and his family moved to England. Twain dealt with his grief by throwing himself into his work. He completed a book called *Following the Equator*, which he based on his lecture tour.

In 1899 the family learned that Jean had epilepsy. Twain took his family to London and to Sweden, where Jean could be treated. Soon, however, they learned that doctors in the United States had begun to treat the disease. By this time, Twain had also paid off his debts. It was time to go home.

Welcome Home

Twain and his family returned to the United States on October 15, 1900. Twain was greeted as a hero. There were press interviews, dinner invitations, and speaking requests. He was now a celebrity. People easily recognized him on the streets. And he was rich again. He was earning up to $100,000 a year for his writings. However his works during this time began to reflect his personal tragedy.

Mark Twain sits in an old rocking chair in this 1906 photograph taken in Dublin, New Hampshire.

Heartbreak

In October 1903, Twain and Livy sailed to Italy. They hoped the climate there would help Livy, who was suffering from heart palpitations and asthma attacks. It did not. On June 5, 1904, Livy died.

Twain was heartbroken. He returned to the United States and again turned to his work for solace. The public had always considered Twain a humorous

Famous One-Liners

Over his lifetime, Twain became famous for a number of creative one-liners, such as these:

- "The difference between the *almost right* word and the *right* word is. . . the difference between the lightning-bug and the lightning."
- "I never told the truth in my life that someone didn't say I was lying, while, on the other hand, I never told a lie that somebody didn't take it as fact."
- "The report of my death has been greatly exaggerated."

satirist. But after Livy's death, his work took on a darker tone. Most of his darkest pieces were not published during his lifetime. In 1908 Twain moved to Redding, Connecticut. The next year, his daughter Jean died of a heart attack from an epileptic seizure.

Literary Legacy

Shortly before Jean's death, Twain began to experience chest pains. After she died, the pains got worse. On April 21, 1910, Mark Twain died of heart failure. More than 3,000 people attended his funeral. The whole country mourned his death.

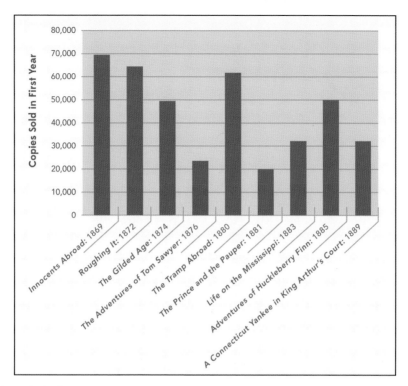

The bar chart is titled with the y-axis label "Copies Sold in First Year" (ranging from 0 to 80,000) and the x-axis categories:

- Innocents Abroad: 1869
- Roughing It: 1872
- The Gilded Age: 1874
- The Adventures of Tom Sawyer: 1876
- The Tramp Abroad: 1880
- The Prince and the Pauper: 1881
- Life on the Mississippi: 1883
- Adventures of Huckleberry Finn: 1885
- A Connecticut Yankee in King Arthur's Court: 1889

Mixed Sales

Twain's books met with different levels of success when they were first released. This graph shows how many copies each book sold during its first year of publication. Compare the first-year sales of *The Adventures of Tom Sawyer* with the sales of *Adventures of Huckleberry Finn*. Why do you think *Huckleberry Finn* was more popular with readers in its first year?

More than 100 years after his death, Twain's literary legacy lives on. Today he is considered the creator of a truly American literature—one that speaks with the voice and language of America.

IMPORTANT DATES

1835
Samuel Langhorne Clemens is born in Florida, Missouri, on November 30.

1839
Clemens moves with his family to Hannibal, Missouri.

1863
Clemens uses the pen name Mark Twain for the first time.

1865
Twain garners nationwide fame with the publication of "Jim Smiley and His Jumping Frog" on November 18.

1870
Twain marries Olivia Langdon on February 2.

1876
The Adventures of Tom Sawyer is published.

1885
Adventures of Huckleberry Finn is published.

1891
Twain and his family move to Europe in an effort to save money on June 6.

1900
Twain and his family return to the United States after nine years abroad on October 15.

1904
Twain's wife Livy dies on June 5.

1910
Twain dies of heart failure at his home in Connecticut on April 21.

KEY WORKS

Adventures of Huckleberry Finn

A novel describing the journey down the Mississippi River made by Huckleberry Finn and a runaway slave named Jim.

Twain, Mark. *Adventures of Huckleberry Finn*. New York: Charles L. Webster, 1885.

The Adventures of Tom Sawyer

A novel of boyhood adventure, based in part on Twain's experiences growing up in Hannibal, Missouri.

Twain, Mark. *The Adventures of Tom Sawyer*. Hartford: American Publishing Co., 1876.

The Gilded Age: A Tale of Today

A novel satirizing political corruption and the American quest for wealth.

Twain, Mark, and Charles Dudley Warner. *The Gilded Age: A Tale of Today*. Hartford: American Publishing Co., 1874.

Life on the Mississippi

An account of Twain's experiences as a steamboat pilot on the Mississippi, along with descriptions of the river's history, science, and folklore.

Twain, Mark. *Life on the Mississippi*. Boston: James R. Osgood, 1883.

The Prince and the Pauper: A Tale for Young People of All Ages

A children's novel in which a prince and a pauper trade places and learn what life is like for the other.

Twain, Mark. *The Prince and the Pauper: A Tale for Young People of All Ages*. Boston: James R. Osgood, 1881.

The Tragedy of Pudd'nhead Wilson

A novel in which a slave boy is raised as the master's son, while the master's son is raised as a slave.

Twain, Mark. *The Tragedy of Pudd'nhead Wilson*. Hartford: American Publishing Co., 1894.

STOP AND THINK

Say What?

Find five words in this book that you have never seen or heard before. Look up what they mean, and rewrite the meanings in your own words. Then write a sentence using each word.

Another View

Ask an adult to help you find another source about slavery. Write a short essay comparing and contrasting its point of view with how slavery is dealt with in *Adventures of Huckleberry Finn*. Be sure to answer these questions: What is the point of view of each author? How are they similar and why? How are they different and why?

Take a Stand

This book discusses journalism and how Mark Twain often exaggerated or made up news stories. Take a position on journalistic honesty. Write a short essay detailing your opinion, reasons for your opinion, and facts and details that support those reasons.

Tell the Tale

This book discusses Mark Twain's experiences as a steamboat pilot. Write 200 words that tell the story of Mark Twain's life on the river. Describe the sights and sounds of the river at night. What is Mark Twain looking out for? What might he be worried about? Set the scene and tell the story.

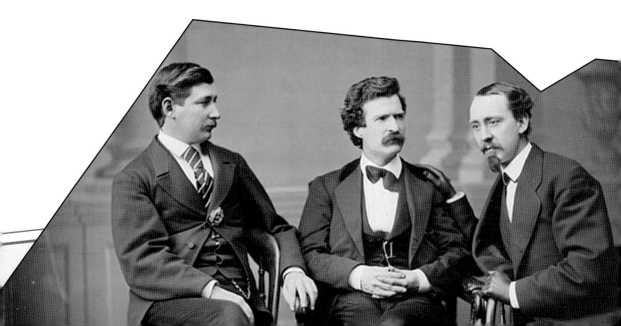

GLOSSARY

apprentice
someone who is learning a
job or trade

autobiographical
having to do with a person's
life story, as told by
that person

diphtheria
a disease that harms the
heart and causes difficulty
breathing, high fever,
and weakness

epilepsy
a disorder that causes
seizures, or uncontrolled
shaking of the body

militia
a military group made up
of people who are not
professional soldiers

pauper
a very poor person

petrified
changed into stone through
minerals and water

rheumatism
a condition in which a
person's joints or muscles
become swollen and sore

satire
a work characterized by the
use of humor or sarcasm to
criticize something

typesetter
someone who arranges
words or letters on a page to
be printed

LEARN MORE

Books

Burleigh, Robert. *The Adventures of Mark Twain by Huckleberry Finn*. New York: Atheneum Books for Young Readers, 2011.

MacLeod, Elizabeth. *Mark Twain: An American Star*. Toronto: Kids Can Press, 2008.

Prince, April Jones. *Who Was Mark Twain?* New York: Grosset & Dunlap, 2004.

Web Links

To learn more about Mark Twain, visit ABDO Publishing Company online at **www.abdopublishing.com.** Web sites about Mark Twain are featured on our Book Links page. These links are routinely monitored and updated to provide the most current information available.

Visit **www.mycorelibrary.com** for free additional tools for teachers and students.

INDEX

ABOUT THE AUTHOR

Valerie Bodden is a freelance author and editor. She has written more than 100 children's nonfiction books. Her books have received many positive reviews. Valerie lives in Wisconsin with her husband and their four children.